The U.S. Armed Forces

The U.S. Navy

by Matt Doeden

Reading Consultant:
Barbara J. Fox
Reading Specialist
North Carolina State University

Capstone press

Mankato, Minnesota

Blazers is published by Capstone Press
151 Good Counsel Drive, P.O. Box 669, Mankato, Minnesota 56002
www.capstonepress.com

Library of Congress Cataloging-in-Publication Data
Doeden, Matt.
   The U.S. Navy / by Matt Doeden.
      p. cm.—(Blazers. The U.S. Armed Forces)
   Includes bibliographical references and index.
   Contents: The U.S. Navy in action—Navy vehicles—Weapons and
equipment—Navy jobs.
      ISBN 0-7368-2737-4 (hardcover)
      1. United States. Navy—Juvenile literature. [1. United States. Navy.]
I. Title.
VA58.4.D64 2005
359'.00973—dc22   2003024301

Editorial Credits

Carrie A. Braulick, editor; Juliette Peters, designer; Jo Miller, photo researcher;
   Eric Kudalis, product planning editor

Photo Credits

Capstone Press/Gary Sundermeyer, cover (inset)
Corbis/Reuters NewMedia Inc., cover
DVIC/General Dynamics Corp., 13 (bottom); JOC Gregg L. Snaza, USN,
   16–17; PH1 William R. Goodwin, USN, 12; PH2 Bunge, USN, 28–29
Folio Inc./Fred J. Moroon, 8–9
Fotodynamics/Ted Carlson, 13 (top)
Getty Images Inc./Justin Sullivan, 7 (bottom); U.S. Navy/James Krogman, 19
U.S. Navy, 20 (bottom); PH1 David C. Lloyd, 27; PH1 James F. Slaughenhaupt,
   20 (top); PH1 Marthaellen L. Ball, 14; PH1 Michael Worner, 22; PH2
   Frederick McCahan, 11; PH2 Inez Lawson, 26; PH3 Jayme T. Pastoric, 15;
   PH3 Philip A. McDaniel, 5, 25; PH3 Yesenia Rosas, 6; PHAN Andre
   Rhoden, 7 (top)

**Capstone Press thanks Mark Wertheimer, historian and curator, Naval Historical
Center, Washington, D.C., for his assistance in preparing this book.**

Table of Contents

The U.S. Navy in Action

An F/A-18 Hornet sits on a Navy aircraft carrier. The plane's engines roar. A catapult holds the plane in place.

Catapult

A crew member signals that the catapult is ready. The catapult pulls the plane forward. The plane soars into the air.

The pilot sees an enemy plane.
He shoots a missile at the plane. The
plane explodes. The aircraft carrier
is safe.

9

Navy Vehicles

Navy members patrol the oceans. They use ships and aircraft.

Cruiser

Cruisers fight enemy ships. Aircraft take off and land on aircraft carriers. Submarines travel underwater. They attack other submarines or land targets.

Aircraft carrier

Submarine

BLAZER FACT

Seawolf submarines are the fastest and quietest submarines in the world.

Seahawk

Navy aircraft fly off aircraft carriers to missions. F-14 Tomcat jets attack targets on the ground. Seahawk helicopters attack targets and lift cargo.

F-14 Tomcat

BLAZER FACT

A catapult can push an F-14 Tomcat to 170 miles (274 kilometers) per hour in less than two seconds.

Aircraft Carrier Diagram

Island

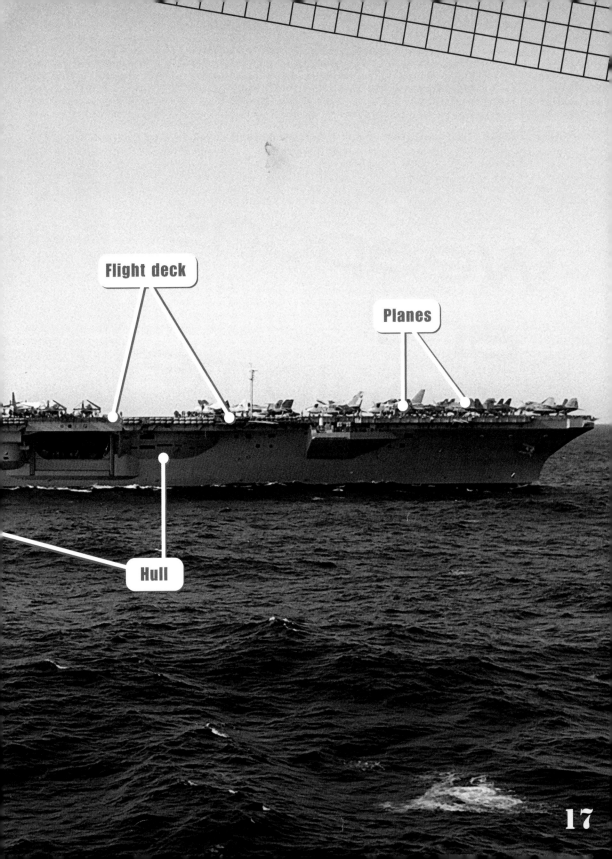

Flight deck

Planes

Hull

Weapons and Equipment

Navy weapons are powerful. Ship crews launch Tomahawk missiles to hit targets on land.

Tomahawk

Harpoon missile

Navy aircraft fire missiles at targets. F/A-18 Hornets fire Harpoon missiles.

Navy members use safety equipment. Sailors are trained to use life vests and lifeboats.

Navy Jobs

Navy crews include ship captains and pilots. The Navy also has mechanics and cooks.

Navy members are enlisted members or officers. Officers have a higher rank than enlisted members. All Navy crews help protect the United States.

NAVY RANKS

★ ★ ★ ★ ★ ★ ★ ★ ★ ★ ★ ★ ★ ★ ★ ★

ENLISTED	**OFFICERS**
Seaman	Ensign
Petty Officer	Lieutenant
	Commander
	Captain
	Admiral

Navy ships travel to a mission

Glossary

aircraft carrier (AIR-kraft KA-ree-ur)—a warship with a large flat deck where aircraft take off and land

captain (CAP-tuhn)—the person in charge of a ship

catapult (KAT-uh-puhlt)—a device that launches aircraft off a ship's flight deck

lifeboat (LYFE-bote)—a small boat carried on a ship for use in an emergency

mechanic (muh-KAN-ik)—a person who fixes machinery

rank (RANGK)—an official position or job level

submarine (SUHB-muh-reen)—a ship that can travel both on the surface and under the water

target (TAR-git)—an object that is aimed at or shot at

Read More

Abramovitz, Melissa. *The U.S. Navy at War.* On the Front Lines. Mankato, Minn.: Capstone Press, 2002.

Bartlett, Richard. *United States Navy.* U.S. Armed Forces. Chicago: Heinemann, 2003.

Green, Michael, and Gladys Green. *The U.S. Navy SEALs at War.* On the Front Lines. Mankato, Minn.: Capstone Press, 2004.

Internet Sites

FactHound offers a safe, fun way to find Internet sites related to this book. All of the sites on FactHound have been researched by our staff.

Here's how:

1. Visit *www.facthound.com*
2. Type in this special code **0736827374** for age-appropriate sites. Or enter a search word related to this book for a more general search.
3. Click on the **Fetch It** button.

FactHound will fetch the best sites for you!

Index